CATHOLIC
READING
A Pilgrimage Trail

Compiled and edited by

John Mullaney and Lindsay Mullaney

Maps and drawings by

John R Mullaney

Scallop Shell Press

ISBN 978-0-9572772-1-2

Published by Scallop Shell Press

29 Derby Road,

Caversham

Reading

RG4 5HE

INTRODUCTION

YEAR OF FAITH 2012 2013

This book has been produced to celebrate the Year of Faith, 2012-2013, announced by Pope Benedict XVI. It was completed just as Pope Francis was elected by the College of Cardinals in March 2013.

Two hundred years ago there were only about 200 Catholics in the Reading area. After the Reformation in the 16th century, to be a Catholic risked facing trial, fines, imprisonment and even death.

Today Reading has nine Catholic churches, five primary schools, a Catholic comprehensive school and a private college. An estimated 4000 Catholics regularly attend Sunday Mass and many more come to church to celebrate major feasts.

This publication coincides with the 175th anniversary of the laying of the foundation stone of Reading's central Catholic church of St James. It is also 200 years since the consecration of the first post-Reformation, purpose-built Catholic chapel in Reading, the Chapel of the Resurrection.

To mark these events, it was decided to produce this book which describes the main places of interest , current and historical, in the story of the Catholic Faith in Reading.

Representatives of all the Reading Catholic parishes have written chapters about their own parishes, with additional information and pictures from other contributors.

The call to go on pilgrimage has been a feature of all major religions, not least Christianity. The word *pilgrimage* originally comes from two Latin words meaning *through the fields*. It evolved to signify a journey to a holy place where the traveller could find a deeper meaning to life. The pilgrim threw himself on the mercy, kindness and generosity of others, sometimes others who did not even share the same language or beliefs.

We hope that by reading this book, and most of all by following the pilgrimage trail, Catholics will discover a new understanding of themselves and their Faith.

These places and stories also hold a wider appeal to those of all faiths, and indeed none, who can learn from them how generosity of spirit and strong principles can overcome affliction and build strong communities.

CONTENTS

Scallop Shell Press

CHAPTER I

A Historic Overview

The Abbey   The Benedictine Abbey in Reading was founded by Henry I in 1121. It was a royal abbey built on royal land, and so under the patronage of the English Crown. The first abbot, Hugh, was appointed in 1123.

Model of the Abbey in Reading Museum.

In 1126 Henry I gave an important relic to the Abbey, namely the hand of St James. So began Reading's association with the pilgrim route to Compostela, in Spain, and its adoption of the emblem of three golden scallop shells on a blue background. The scallop shells still decorate the coat of arms of Reading University.

With the death of Henry I, in 1135, civil war broke out between his daughter Matilda and his nephew Stephen. In 1150 a castle was constructed within the

Abbey grounds and the Forbury Hill may be the site of its remains. Henry was buried in Reading Abbey in 1136. By 1164 the Abbey church was completed and Thomas à Becket, Archbishop of Canterbury, consecrated the church.

Henry II was present for this ceremony. Within six years, Henry, according to popular belief, was to order the murder of Thomas, his erstwhile friend.

Over the next 400 years the town of Reading and its Abbey grew in influence and importance.

On several occasions the Royal Court and Parliament met in Reading. As a centre of pilgrimage and trade, both the town and the Abbey prospered. To accommodate more travellers, and to care for the needy, the Hospitium, near St. Lawrence's, was enlarged towards the end of the 12th century. In 1485 a grammar school was founded in the Hospitium.

The Dissolution of the Abbey

Four hundred years of Catholic worship in Reading Abbey came to an end in 1539.

Henry VIII dissolved the Abbey and executed its Abbot, Hugh Cook of Faringdon. Some of the Abbey buildings were allocated for royal use.

Part of the Hospitium was converted into stables for the King's horses. With the accession of Edward VI in 1547, the systematic destruction of the Abbey began in earnest. Some stones were used in the Minster church of St Mary; others were taken to London and Windsor.

The stained glass and paving tiles were all sold off. Over the next 200 years, what was left became available as a quarry for builders in and around Reading. In 1560, two years after Elizabeth I came to the throne, she granted Reading a charter. This was the basis of Reading's administrative system for the next 300 years and even has implications for today's Borough Council.

The Mayor and burgesses became the governing body of the town with all the rights and duties which that entailed.

Abbot Hugh Cook of Faringdon.

They also became responsible for education, the maintenance of the roads and bridges and the administration of justice.

They could enforce by-laws governing the conduct of trade, including overseeing weights and measures.

The Charter made specific mention of the fact that nineteen of the many bridges in Reading were 'very ruinous'.

The Queen gave her permission for '200 loads of stones' from the Abbey to be used for their reconstruction.

Evidence of this is still visible today.

The Civil War and its Aftermath

The Civil War had the next significant impact on the Abbey ruins: one which was to affect the story of Catholicism in Reading 200 years later.

In 1643 Reading was a Royalist stronghold under a Catholic governor, Sir Arthur Aston. To strengthen the defences of the town he built several fortifications in strategic positions around Reading, including on the Forbury mound.

The Abbey Ruins
The dormitory was on the upper level.

According to some sources Aston placed a cannon here to command and defend the eastern approaches, but since some of the Abbey ruins were in the line of fire he set a mine and blew them up. Some of these remains can still be seen today alongside St James' Church. This story may be apocryphal but the huge blocks are certainly fallen masonry from the Abbey church.

Following the Civil War and the Restoration of the Monarchy, Reading became an ever greater stronghold of various Protestant sects. In the 19th century the Quaker movement, for example, proved an exceptional influence on Reading's main industries of beer, biscuits and seeds. The town became synonymous with the names of Simonds, Palmer and Sutton as they expanded their businesses and gave employment to the people of Reading.

Huntley and Palmer biscuit factory complex in 19th century Reading

Courtesy of Reading Library

The Return of Legal Catholicism

From the 1580s the anti-Papist laws had made it difficult for Catholics openly to go to Mass. One record shows that there were only a few, maybe just 40 or so, Catholics in Reading in the middle of the 18th century.

In contrast to this, many of the great country estates around the town belonged to Catholic families. The Englefields owned the Whiteknights Estate, the Perkins owned Ufton Court, and the Blounts held Mapledurham.

The gradual relaxation of the anti-Catholic penal laws, culminating in the 1791 Catholic Relief Act and the 1829 Catholic Emancipation Act, allowed Catholics once again to play a full role in the life of the nation and so of the town.

This booklet looks at those places which hold special significance for Catholics: places which tell a story spanning nearly one thousand years from the founding of the Abbey to today's thriving parish communities. The stones of Reading speak to us across the centuries and tell of a journey of faith, a pilgrimage trail, which carries a message for our lives today.

Allow at least 2 hours.
Walking times are given for each stage,
over the following pages.

Red dots - Central Reading
Pilgrimage Trail.

Green dots - The Blessed
Hugh Faringdon Trail.
See pages 48 –49.

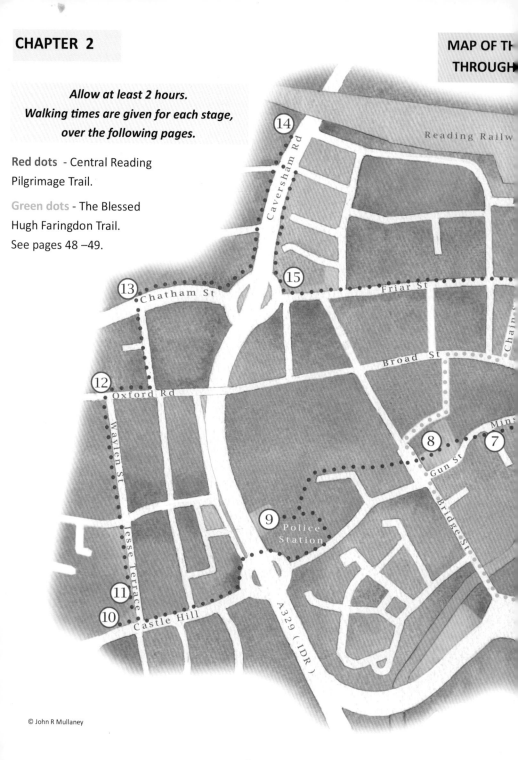

© John R Mullaney

KEY

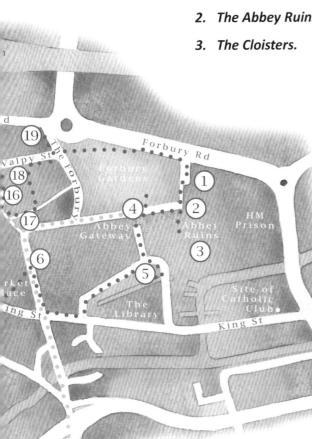

1. St James' Church, presbytery and school.

2. The Abbey Ruins and Abbots Walk.

3. The Cloisters.

4. The Forbury, the memorial cross to Henry I and the Abbey Gateway.

5. The Abbey Mill.

6. Market Place and the Mercury Offices.

7. Minster Street.

8. St Mary's Minster.

9. Site of Finch's Buildings.

10. The French Priests' House.

11. Site of the Convent School.

12. Holy Trinity Church.

13. The Irish Centre.

14. Blessed Dominic Barberi plaque.

15. Greyfriars Church.

16. Reading Museum.

17. St Lawrence's Church.

18. The Hospitium.

19. The Rising Sun public house and the site of the Chapel of the Resurrection.

1. The Shrine of St James in St James' Church.

The Start of the Pilgrimage

WALK MAP   *Stages 1 - 5.*   *Allow 25 minutes walking time.*

1. St James' Church. 2. Abbots Walk and the Abbey Ruins. 3. The Cloisters. 4. Site of the execution of Abbot Hugh Cook of Faringdon, the memorial cross to Henry I and the Abbey Gateway. 5. The Abbey Mill Arch.

1. St. James' Church

Designed by A.W.N. Pugin and built on land owned by James Wheble, it was opened in 1840. Wheble also financed its construction.

See pages 24 and 25 for further details.

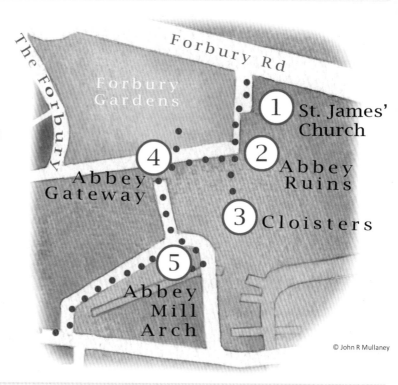

© John R Mullaney

Facing the main door to St James' Church, turn right. Start your walk by following the small pathway which separates the Forbury Gardens, on your right, from the church, the presbytery and the nursery school, which are on your left.

Education has always been important to Catholic life. St James' School was built in 1876 and served the Catholic community until after the Second World War when it moved to *Christ the King* in Whitley. It was a Catholic nursery school for some years in the 1970s and '80s before becoming a private nursery.

You are now walking across the main transept of the old Abbey. If you look closely at the wall on your right you will see some stones from the Abbey. Look even more closely and you may spot one with a cross carved on it.

2. Abbots Walk

After passing under the stone gateway, enter into Abbots Walk, turn left, go to the railings and look at the Abbey Ruins.

This has been a sacred site for nearly 1000 years.

Frederic Cowslade and his family lived in no. 12 from the late 1840s. Frederic was the owner of the *Reading Mercury* newspaper and grandson of Mrs Smart who was so instrumental in bringing Catholicism back to Reading in the late 18th century.

Abbots Walk and The Abbey Ruins

3. The Cloisters

Go down Abbots Walk, take the first left and go behind the houses.

Here you will find a green space. Though not exactly in the same place as the Abbey Cloisters, their spirit has been beautifully recreated in this peaceful spot.

4. The Abbey Gateway

Retracing your steps into Abbots Walk, turn left towards the Abbey Gateway.

At the Gateway enter the Forbury Gardens by the right-hand entrance.

To your right you will see a large stone cross. This is a memorial to Henry I, who founded the Abbey in 1121.

This is not the site of his burial, which most likely was in front of the high altar, approximately where the school now stands. The cross is near the site of the west front of the great Abbey church.

It was somewhere near here that the last Abbot, Hugh Cook of Faringdon, was hanged, drawn and quartered, along with two other priests: John Eynon the priest in charge of St Giles, and John Rugge. (See Chapter 12)

Henry VIII intended the execution as a deliberate act of public humiliation, not just of the Abbot but of the monastery, its monks and all who maintained their loyalty to the old Faith and to Rome.

This was a most brutal form of execution. It is worth taking a moment, as you look across the calm of the Forbury Gardens to the church of St. James, to remember these terrible events and the martyrdom of these priests.

Retrace your steps and pass through the Abbey Gateway.

The Abbey Gateway has suffered much over the years. It collapsed in the 19th century and was restored by the great Victorian architect, George Gilbert Scott.

It was also the site of the school attended by Jane Austen.

In the 20th century the Catholics of St. James' used it as a community meeting room and social club.

Finding your next stopping place may present a slight challenge. But in the spirit of true pilgrims seek out the way. Go through the Abbey Gateway into Abbey Street, follow the road down, first to the left then bear right, until you see the Holy Brook on your right.

5. The Abbey Mill Arch

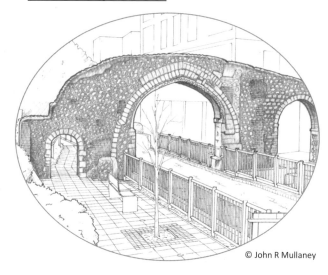

© John R Mullaney

The drawing above shows what you are looking for.

Milling and bread were as important in medieval times as they are today.

The mill was in use until 1959.

Bread has a special significance to Christians. Perhaps reflecting on the words of the *Our Father*, also known as the *Lord's Prayer,* would be an appropriate meditation in this secluded spot in the middle of commercial Reading.

Give us our daily bread and forgive us as we forgive others.

Retrace you steps to Abbey Street. Turn left and, bearing left, follow the road round until you get to the Library. On reaching the main road, Kings Road, turn right until you come to the High Street. Turn right into Market Place.

WALK MAP
Stages 6 - 9.

Allow 30 minutes walking time.

6. The Mercury offices.

7. Minster Street.

8. Saint Mary's Minster Church.

9. Finch's Buildings.

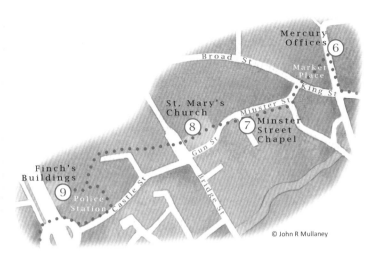

© John R Mullaney

6. The Mercury Offices

In the centre of the pedestrian area, stand by the Simeon Monument, designed by the famous architect Sir John Soane. Look around until you see the building called Soane Point. You are facing the site of the offices of the Reading Mercury newspaper.

From 1762 the owner and editor of *The Mercury* was Anna Maria Smart, the Catholic wife of the poet Christopher Smart.

With her daughters, Marianne and Elizabeth, she was responsible for bringing the first five French émigré priests to Reading, in 1792—3, smuggling them through the streets of the town to their new place of refuge in Finch's Buildings.

Marianne married Thomas Cowslade and the paper stayed in the hands of the Cowslade family until 1915.

When she died, in 1809, Mrs Smart's obituary said she was "*A Catholic in religion, a Christian in true spirit of the character,* who *never enquired the principles of anyone who solicited her help.*"

In the 1840's Marianne's daughter, Ellenor, wrote an account of the early years of the Catholic church in Reading.

Known as the *Cowslade Manuscript*, it is a major source of information about Reading's Catholic community in the late 18th and early 19th centuries.

The Reading Mercury offices are the third shop front on the right.
Courtesy—Reading Library.

11

Leave Market Place by the narrow pedestrian road on the right. Go straight across into Minster Street. Walk under the archway and along Minster Street until you come to the back entrance of the John Lewis store.

7. Minster Street Secret Chapel.

Before it became legal for Catholics to attend Mass, Mrs Smart rented a room somewhere in Minster Street. Here Father Baynham, a Franciscan priest, came from Whiteknights to say Mass in secret.

According to Ellenor Cowslade, on one occasion, her aunt, Elizabeth Smart, arriving to prepare for Mass, was told by the landlord that he would not allow the priest to 'perform' because his wife was in labour. Elizabeth bravely continued her preparations and the Mass:

went on without interruption beyond the sound of vessels being emptied with the accompaniment of offensive smells.

Following this incident Elizabeth, who had received some money as a legacy,

Minster Street, c. 1820

resolved to find a permanent place where Mass could be held.

Continue along Minster Street and enter St. Mary's Churchyard.

8. The Minster Church of St Mary

Dating from Saxon times St Mary's was largely rebuilt and extended after the Reformation. Some of the stone and timber used for this reconstruction came from the ruined Abbey. It is claimed that the pillars separating the south aisle from the nave were from this source, as well as the north door.

The churchyard contains the graves of at least six of the French priests who came to Reading during the Revolution. There are records of nine of these priests being buried or having a funeral here between 1797 and 1804.

© John R Mullaney

St. Mary's Minster Church

9. Finch's Buildings

Leave the churchyard and cross the Butts to enter Hosier Street, with the market area to your left. Now walk towards the Hexagon theatre. To the left of the entrance take the ramp and look down into the garden area and across to the IDR.

Somewhere near here is the site of Finch's Buildings, also known as Lady Vachel's House.

This tenement building was demolished during the development of the IDR in the 1960s but it played a most important part in the return of Catholicism to Reading. This was the house bought, or possibly leased, in 1791, by Elizabeth Smart, so that Mass could be said for the Catholics of the town. The Mass once more became legal after the 1791 Catholic Relief Act

When, in 1792, the French Revolutionary Assembly required all priests in France to swear allegiance to the new Constitution, thousands of French clergy were forced to leave France and seek exile abroad.

Mrs Smart and her daughters, Marianne and Elizabeth, heard of four priests from the diocese of Rouen who were waiting in Dover for an offer of refuge and wrote, inviting them to Reading. They came to live in Finch's Buildings. The house became a presbytery and chapel, which was furnished with fittings and vestments from the Whiteknights estate.

The names of these four original priests were the Abbés Loriot, Miard de la Blardière, Godquin and Gondré. They made their living by teaching French and Latin in the town.

In 1802 they were joined by the young priest, François Longuet, who was to prove so important to the Catholic life of Reading.

Finch's Buildings just before their demolition.
Courtesy of Reading Library

Retrace your steps for about 30 yards, turn right and head for the Magistrates' Court. Take the footpath between the Courts and the Police Station. Turn right and walk towards the roundabout. Keeping to the right, cross the dual-carriageway and, at the Salvation Army building, walk up Castle Hill. On your right, before the traffic lights, and opposite the Register Office, you will find a large white building with two side wings and a big cedar of Lebanon tree in front of it.

WALK MAP Stages 10 - 15.

Allow 35 minutes walking time.

10. The French Priests' House.

11. The Convent.

12. Holy Trinity Church.

13. The Irish Centre.

14. Blessed Dominic Barberi Plaque.

15. Greyfriars Church.

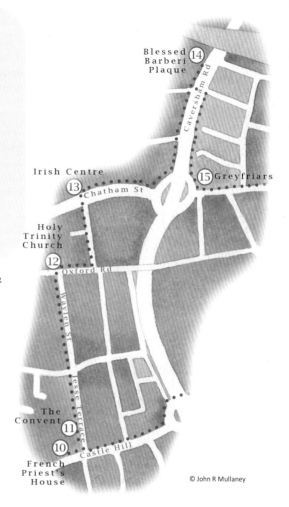

© John R Mullaney

10. The French Priests' House, Castle Hill.

In 1796 the British government requisitioned this old coaching inn to house large numbers of French priests, mainly from Normandy. They had been living, with hundreds more French clergy, in the King's House, Winchester, but this was now needed as barracks for troops in the war against France. About 350 priests were based in the house, although some of them had lodgings in the town.

The house had a large chapel, probably in the old ballroom of the hotel, and the people of Reading must have become used to seeing the priests streaming up Castle Hill to their Divine Office services several times a day.

Ellenor Cowslade remembered attending Benediction in the chapel as a small child and *being commended as a good little girl for having been quiet and orderly during the long service.*

The late 18th century illustration opposite shows an engraving of the house as it then was, with a colonnaded frontage giving the impression of a cloister and formal flowerbeds in front of the building. Around one of the beds are the words *Rooted by Gratitude.*

These words probably refer to the cedar of Lebanon we see today, planted as a sapling by the French priests.

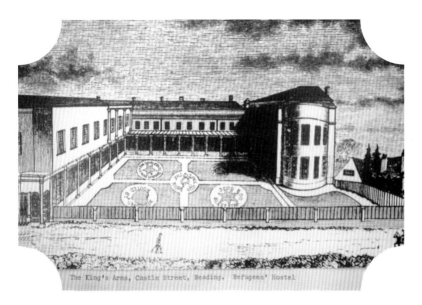

The King's Arms, Castle Street, Reading. Refugees' Hostel

Behind the house was a cemetery where those priests who died in Reading were buried. There is no trace of it today and it is unclear what happened to these graves. Possibly the remains were removed and taken back to France when the priests returned there in 1802, after Napoleon came to power and restrictions on the clergy were relaxed. The house was then returned to private ownership.

To the right of the house as you face it is a terrace of houses. This was the site of the Convent.

11. The Convent

In the late 18th and early 19th century this area became one of Reading's centres for schools and places of tuition. Possibly the most famous was Mrs Jesse's school.

In December 1901 the Sisters of St. Marie Madeleine Postel moved from Bracknell to Reading. They rented two houses of a block of five in Jesse Terrace.

During the Christmas holidays the sisters worked to prepare the rooms for the school which they were able to open on the 16th of January 1902.

The reputation of the school spread and the number of students increased. In 1905 The Round House, formerly the Kings Arms Inn, (the French Priests' House), adjoining the block of five, was added to the Convent. As the Castle Hill site was limited for development of the growing school and the rent was expensive, the sisters searched for a more suitable property.

In March 1909 Broad Oak House, Upper Redlands Road, came up for sale and the school moved from Castle Hill in September 1910.

In 1907 two sisters from the Convent taught in the little school next to St. James' Church. The sisters received no salary directly, but the services of the clergy to the Convent were gratis. The conditions in the old parish school were so bad that two sisters caught typhoid and died, one in 1911 and the other in 1913. Much to their regret the sisters were withdrawn from St. James' School in 1919.

Walk back towards town but take the first left, Jesse Terrace. Admire the elegant architecture of so many of the buildings.

Carry straight down Waylen Street. On your left you will pass the central Jamme Masjid mosque. When you reach the Oxford Road you will see Holy Trinity Church on the other side.

12. Holy Trinity Church.

Pugin was undoubtedly one of Catholicism's greatest architects in the 19th century. We are fortunate, in Reading, to have his very first church design, St James' in the Forbury. But there is another connection.

The rood screen that Pugin designed for St Chad's, Birmingham, found its way to Reading in the late 20th century thanks to Canon Brindley, who saved it from the scrap-yard when the authorities at St Chad's discarded it.

Pugin's Rood Screen, transferred from St Chad's Birmingham to Holy Trinity, Reading
Coyright George Landow   www. victorianweb.org

A rood screen was a common feature in late medieval churches. It was the partition, often ornate, between the chancel and nave.

Of more or less open tracery it was made of wood, stone, or wrought iron, surmounted by a rood loft carrying the Great Rood, a sculptural representation of the Crucifixion.

The church is open at certain times but to visit it contact the churchwardens.

13. The Irish Centre

The Centre was opened in 1987 by the Mayor, Mrs Lawrence. The club has been not just a centre for Irish and Catholics, but, in traditional Irish fashion, a place of welcome, fun and companionship for all Reading people. Its importance in the community was underlined with the visit in 2010 of Mary McAleese, then President of Ireland.

Irish people and their priests were the backbone of many of the emerging Catholic parishes and schools in Reading during the 20th century.

As you face the church turn right and walk towards Reading. Very soon turn left into Eaton Place. Walk down this road with the multi-storey car park to your right until you come to Chatham Street. Cross this dual carriageway and to your left is the Irish Centre.

Facing the entrance to the Centre turn right towards Reading via the narrow pathway with a grass verge on your right. Follow the pedestrian path across a small access road, keeping to the left where it splits, until you emerge at a roundabout. Over the dual carriageway you can see Greyfriars Church. Turn left until you come to the traffic lights on Great Knollys Street. The building you are looking for is the second block on your left.

14. Blessed Dominic Barberi Plaque

The plaque on this modern block of flats marks the site of an inn called the *Railway Tavern*.

On the 27th of August 1849 the Passionist missionary priest, Dominic Barberi, was brought here from Reading Railway Station, having been taken ill on the train between Reading and Pangbourne. He died, probably of heart failure, that same afternoon. Dominic Barberi, who was beatified in 1963, is best known for having received Cardinal

Blessed Dominic Barberi
1792 - 1849

John Henry Newman, himself beatified in 2011 into the Catholic Church in October 1845.

Newman, Wiseman, Faber and other prominent churchmen often turned to him for advice.

Originally coming from Pallanzana, just north of Rome, Dominic Barberi was ordained as a Passionist priest in 1818. Despite his lack of English he always felt that his vocation was as a missionary in England.

Eventually he was able to set up a community at Stone in Staffordshire.

Despite great opposition he gradually won round the local people and was able to open a school and church designed by Pugin.

Increasingly, Dominic's work consisted in giving parish missions all over England, despite his poor English and a severe stutter which, however, almost disappeared when he was preaching.

The Railway Tavern c. 1840
Courtesy of Reading Library

He made many hundreds of converts and was highly regarded by both Catholics and many Protestants. In 1847, when the re-establishment of the Hierarchy was being discussed, it was suggested that Dominic should become Bishop of Reading. Sadly, he died before the Hierarchy was re-established and Reading never got its Catholic Bishop.

Retrace your steps to Great Knollys Street and cross over the road.
Make your way up the Caversham Road (alongside of the dual carriageway)
until you come to Greyfriars Church

15 Greyfriars Church

Often described as the oldest church in Reading, this was a Franciscan friary, founded in 1311.

At the Dissolution of the Monasteries, in 1538, it was surrendered to the crown. The building fell into disrepair and its contents were plundered by local people.

In the years that followed, the Franciscans continued to work in secret, based at the homes of local Catholic families: at Whiteknights, Ufton Court and Mapledurham.

One of them, Father Baynham, occasionally came to say Mass in the chapel in Minster Street before the Mass centre at Finch's Buildings was opened.

After leaving Whiteknights, Father Baynham lived a poor and simple life at Ufton Court. He was one of the first priests in the country to take advantage of the 1791 Act which permitted legal places of worship to Catholics.

He continued to serve the community until his death in 1803 after which the French priests at Finch's Buildings took over his duties.

The dilapidated church itself was used successively as a guildhall, a workhouse and a prison. The picture shows how men and women were separated by a wall across the nave. Eventually, in 1863, the building was restored and become an Anglican church. Today, Greyfriars is home to a thriving evangelical Anglican church.

Much of the medieval stonework and the fine decorated style west window can still be seen, although a modern extension replaces the original west end.

Greyfriars c. 1816
Courtesy of Reading Library

The Franciscans

The story of how the rich young man, Giovanni di Bernadone, turned his back on luxury and wealth and became known to the world as St. Francis, is well known throughout the world.

Born in Assisi in central Italy towards the end of the 12th century, Francis gathered a group of like minded people around him. The community was recognised by the Pope as a religious order and its appeal to simplicity and love of nature spread rapidly through Europe.

So it came about that during the middle ages many towns had a group of Franciscan *friars,* (from the Latin *fratres,* meaning *brothers*). Their habits were of the cheapest fabric, brown or grey, in contrast to the Benedictines' black. Consequently they became known as *Greyfriars*. They earned their living through preaching and relying on gifts from the people and were known as *mendicant* or *begging friars*. Though some friaries became rich, the simple philosophy of Francis persisted. His own lack of ambition is reflected in the fact that he himself was never ordained as a priest. He remained a simple friar all his life.

Perhaps his most popular and lasting legacy is the idea of telling the Christmas story through the images of the crib.

As we look on this ancient *friary* or *brothers' house*, take time to meditate on one of the verses from St Francis' great poem *The Canticle of the Sun*.

Be praised, my Lord, through our sister Mother Earth, who feeds us and rules us, and produces so many fruits with their multi-coloured flowers and leaves.

St Francis by Giotto

A medieval Franciscan friar

The End of the Reading Pilgrimage Trail

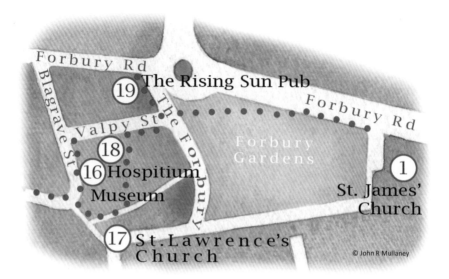

© John R Mullaney

WALK MAP　　　　　**Stages 16 – 19**　　　*Allow 30 minutes walking time.*

16. Reading Museum and junction of Valpy St and Blagrave St (one of the possible sites of the *Chapel of the Resurrection*).

17. St Lawrence's Church.

18. The Hospitium.

19. The Rising Sun Public House (traditional site of the *Chapel of the Resurrection*).

1. St James' Church - the shrine to St James, patron saint of pilgrims, and the end of the Reading Pilgrimage Trail.

From Greyfriars walk down Friar Street, which still records, by its name, the presence of the Franciscan friars, towards the fine Town Hall designed in the 19th century by Alfred Waterhouse, the architect of the Natural History Museum in London. When you reach the Old Town Hall, cross the road, turn left and walk past the Museum entrance to the corner of Valpy Street and Blagrave Street.

This is one of the possible locations where the *Chapel of the Resurrection* and the priest's house stood from 1811 to 1840. (See page 22)

Walk back to the Museum. If you have the time a visit would be very worth while.

16 Reading Museum

The first entrance, to the left, in Blagrave Street, leads to Reading's excellent museum.

In it you will find a model of the Abbey and an exhibition area which clearly shows the various buildings and their relationship with the town. You will be able to admire some of the beautiful surviving architectural masterpieces from the Abbey: column capitals and pieces of sculpture, as well as other very informative displays.

Walk back past the Museum. At the statue of Queen Victoria turn left to reach St. Lawrence's church. On either side of the main doors you will see two sets of coats of arms. One shows the town's crest, the other the scallop shells of St James.

17. St Lawrence's Church

The original church was built in Saxon times, to the north of its present site.

St Lawrence's Church and Market Place c 1800

It was demolished, to make way for the Hospitium, and rebuilt in the 12th century, and became the town's parish church, served by the Abbey but not part of it.

Next to St Lawrence's was the gate through which pilgrims, who would mainly arrive down what is now London Street, entered the Abbey precincts. After the dissolution of the monastery St Lawrence's fell into such a state of decay that in 1547 it was taken down and rebuilt, using some of the original structure. Its roof is said to date from 1410.

Today the church is used for youth ministry and the interior has been largely remodelled. Unfortunately it is not normally open to visitors.

As an aside it should be noted that the spelling has varied. Sometimes it was spelt *St Lawrence,* with a *'w',* at other times *St Laurence* with a *'u'.*

Go down the passage way to the left of St Lawrence's and enter the churchyard. Turn left after a few yards and take the path to the Hospitium. Go round the building into a courtyard with a bronze sculpture of three figures.

18. The Hospitium

Originally the whole building was designed to house pilgrims coming to visit the Abbey and its relics, especially the hand of St James.

The Abbey offered two free days of board and lodging to pilgrims.

Under King Henry VII the upper floor of the Hospitium was converted into a grammar school, the forerunner of Reading School, whilst the lower floor was retained as a dormitory for pilgrims. With the dissolution of Reading Abbey the dormitory was converted into stables.

Make your way though the archway into Valpy Street, turn right then cross over and follow the road round until you reach the Rising Sun Public House.

19. The Rising Sun Public House

For 150 years this has been the reputed site of the *Chapel of the Resurrection,* although recent research has thrown some doubt on its location.

Nevertheless, somewhere close to here, the French émigré priest, Father François Longuet, bought a house and built a chapel for the Catholics of Reading. This was the first purpose built Catholic chapel in Reading since the Reformation.

Father Longuet was murdered, in February 1817, on the Oxford Road while returning from Wallingford. He was buried in his chapel but when St James' was built in 1840 his remains were transferred and buried at the foot of the high altar.

1. Saint James' Church

Your pilgrimage is almost at an end. Cross over the road into the Forbury Gardens. You can either go back to Abbots Walk or take the Forbury Road and make your way to St James' Church.

The Shrine of Saint James

On reaching the church look up at the bell. This was first sounded in August 1840. It was the first time since the Reformation that the sound of a Catholic church bell was heard in Reading.

In monastic tradition the sound of the bell is called the *voice of God: vox Dei.*

Enter the church and visit the shrine to the patron saint of pilgrims, St James.

Memorial plaque to Father François Longuet

Inside the church, in front of the altar, you can see the memorial plaque put in place in 1840 to commemorate this remarkable French priest who had escaped from Revolutionary France, was ordained in England and gave his life to the new mission in Reading.

Perhaps in the manner and custom of pilgrims for hundreds of years, you may wish to light a candle and take time to reflect on whatever meaning this day's pilgrimage has brought to you.

CHAPTER 3

St James' in The Forbury.
Pugin's Most Beautiful Church on the Way of the Pilgrims

On the 14th of December 1837 there occurred the most significant event in the history of Catholicism in Reading since the Reformation. On land donated to the Catholic Church, by James Wheble, of Woodley, the foundation stone of St James' Church was laid by the notable Victorian architect, A.W.N. Pugin, a convert to the Catholic faith.

The Catholic bishop of the London District, Thomas Griffiths, presided, and, after a sermon given by Father James O'Neil, the Bishop's chaplain, the ground on which the church was to be built was sprinkled with holy water. Prayers were said at the four points of the building's foundations.
A throng, estimated by the *Reading Mercury* news paper at between two and three thousand people, attended the ceremony.

The church was completed in 1840. It was solemnly opened by the Bishop on August 5th. He returned to consecrate the altar on November 28th.

There have been two later additions to the building. The Lady Chapel and the Sacristy were added in 1926 and the north aisle in 1962.

The latter extension does not conform with Pugin's original architectural vision.

However you can admire the original Pugin roof vaulting, the 19th century stained glass above the altar and the recent decoration, in the style of Pugin, in the sanctuary and the Lady Chapel.

Surprisingly for Pugin, who usually worked in the neo-Gothic style, St James' is a Norman–Romanesque building, so designed to be sympathetic to the period of the ancient Abbey.

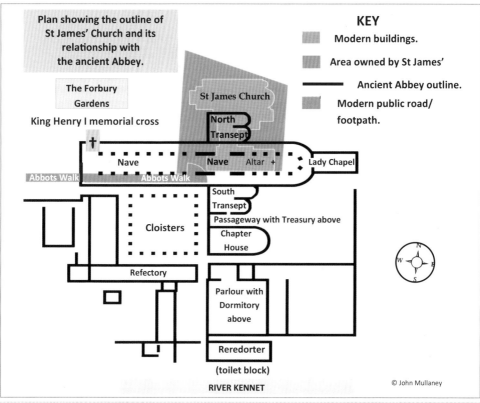

KEY

- Modern buildings.
- Area owned by St James'
- Ancient Abbey outline.
- Modern public road/ footpath.

Plan showing the outline of St James' Church and its relationship with the ancient Abbey.

The Forbury Gardens

King Henry I memorial cross

St James Church

North Transept

Nave | Nave | Altar + | Lady Chapel

Abbots Walk

South Transept

Passageway with Treasury above

Cloisters

Chapter House

Refectory

Parlour with Dormitory above

Reredorter (toilet block)

RIVER KENNET

© John Mullaney

St James' Church stands just to the north of the old Abbey church.
The diagram above shows the relationship between the two buildings.
The location of the altar, marked with a cross, is approximate.

François Longuet
1771 - 1817
Founder of the Chapel of the Resurrection

Reading Catholics owe a great debt of gratitude to these two French émigré priests.

Forsaking the land of their birth, they ministered to the emerging Catholic community.

Let us remember the sacrifices they made so that we today can benefit from their time labouring in the vineyard of the Church.

Miard de la Blardière
1760 - c. 1841
Chaplain to James Wheble

Today's Church

As you look around remember that the church is not just about its history, about the past. It is here for you and all around you.

The church works in and for the community. Over 600 people regularly come each weekend to Mass at St James'. They represent more than 60 nations. It is a busy centre for many activities but above all it is a place of peace and rest in the pilgrimage through life.

A parishioner recently wrote this meditation on entering the church.

Central window over the High Altar

When I enter the church, before me straight down the main aisle, I see the Sanctuary and the Altar and a great wave of spiritual emotion crashes over me: I feel that I have come home and that I am in the presence of God. I know too that I am in a Holy place and my soul is nourished and lightened. Oft times, whilst singing the Gloria *or the* Agnus Dei, *I feel the spirits of all the people, the monks, the earlier parishioners who have worshipped in this Holy and Blessed place, alongside, raising their voices with mine in the praise of God.*

Sanctuary with new crucifix by the Brazilian artist, Guilherme Marques

This is indeed a Holy Place.

For 400 years it was the site of a revered monastery and finally the home of the last abbot, a holy martyr of the Church, Blessed Hugh Faringdon.

Today it is a sanctuary in the centre of a busy town. It is also a stopping place for pilgrims on their way to Santiago in Spain.

For you, a pilgrim in Reading, it has been the starting and finishing point of your own pilgrimage trail.

CHAPTER 4

St William of York and Area

Leave your car in St. William of York's parking area, if open, otherwise use the road .

The Church

The church was built in 1906 by Father William le Grave, a retired Army chaplain, who had volunteered to do missionary work. It was the third Catholic church to be built in the Reading area since the Reformation, after the Chapel of the Resurrection and St James'. Father le Grave was a proud Yorkshireman, which may explain the dedication to St William of York.

Father le Grave built the church with his own money, plus generous help from the wealthy Lonergan family. For many years, from 1880 onwards, the Lonergans had provided access to their private chapel for local Catholics, but at that time it was well outside the built up area of Reading. In contrast St William's was well sited to serve a densely built area.

The annex on the east side of St William was built in 1958 thanks to another generous benefactor, Miss Muriel Bowman-Smith.

As well as its regular congregation, St William's is used for Reading University chaplaincy Masses during term time.

Turn right out of the car park and walk along Redlands Rd until you reach the entrance to St. Joseph's College.

There has been an independent Catholic school on this site since 1910, when the Sisters of Saint Marie Madeleine Postel moved from Castle Hill. Until 2010 it was St Joseph's Convent School for girls. Today it is an independent Catholic school for boys and girls aged 3 to 18.

Retrace your steps to St William's.

Across the road from St William's, at Number 29, is the new home of the Catholic Chaplaincy. This used to be the priest's house until the retirement of the last parish priest.

Walk along Upper Redlands Road to its east end, where it meets Eastern Avenue (to the left) and Whiteknights Road (branching right).

At this junction, a gate to the right leads into the University's Whiteknights campus, an important place of Catholic worship in the 18th century when the Englefield family owned Whiteknights.

The chapel furniture was moved in the 18th century to Finch's Buildings and later to the Chapel of the Resurrection.

Walk down Eastern Avenue. The house at number 45 was the home of Father le Grave. It was used as a Mass centre in the period 1904 - 1906 before St. William's was built.

CHAPTER 5

The Parish of Our Lady and St Anne, Caversham

Caversham in the Middle Ages

Caversham Catholics have a spiritual heritage of which they may well be proud. The name of Caversham first emerged soon after the Norman Conquest, when the Manor of Caversham was granted by William the Conqueror to Walter Gifford, Earl of Buckingham. In 1162, he founded Notley Abbey in Buckinghamshire for the Augustinian Canons. As part of the endowment of the new Abbey, Gifford granted them the church of St. Peter in Caversham and the Shrine of Our Lady which may have been sited where Dean's Farm stands today. Thus began a long and intimate connection between Caversham and the canons of St. Augustine, which ended only with the Reformation.

Caversham Bridge

The ecclesiastical importance of Caversham began in the middle of the 13th century with the building of a bridge to Caversham by the monks of Reading Abbey. In medieval times a bridge sometimes incorporated a chapel. These chapels were often built by the many guilds as part of their charitable work. A chaplain to the guild would have been present at the chapel to pray each morning for the safety of travellers. In Caversham there were two small adjoining chapels standing on an island in the middle of the river, dedicated respectively to Our Lady and to St. Anne.

In 1538 Thomas Cromwell sent Dr London to dismantle the Shrine. Its chapel was razed to the ground.

When today's Caversham Bridge was built in 1924 several pieces of stonework, believed to be the foundations of a bridge chapel, were unearthed. These were given to the parish of Our Lady and St. Anne and used in the construction of the restored shrine adjacent to St. Anne's Church. Today, a plaque on the bridge acknowledges: *The little chapel on the great bridge 1231 – 1500.*

St. Anne's Church and the Shrine.

The parish of Our Lady and St. Anne was established in 1896 thanks largely to the generosity of Mrs. Florence Crawshay, who lived in Caversham Park, now home to the BBC Monitoring Service. She invited a group of French Sisters of Mercy to come and live in Caversham. The Crawshays provided the Sisters with a property in Southview Avenue called The Firs. The Chapel of the new convent was blessed in 1896 by the Bishop of Birmingham. The first public Mass was celebrated on Low Sunday, 1896 in the newly formed parish of Our Lady and St. Anne, named to recall the former shrine of Our Lady of Caversham and the chapel of St. Anne. In 1898 Dr. Cockran, a generous benefactor to the parish, purchased the site of the present church and school. In 1902 the foundation stone of the present church was laid.

The following year the presbytery was built. and the church was extended to accommodate the growing number of parishioners.

Mrs. Crawshay endowed the church with a high altar, organ and vestments. She also presented what became known as the Lady Altar and a beautiful, Italian 18th century, white marble statue of Our Lady. The statue was regarded as the renewed statue of Our Lady of Caversham for over forty years until it was transferred to the chapel dedicated to Our Lady of Caversham which was built in Richmond Road, Caversham Heights in 1954. With the closure of the chapel in 1999, the statue was brought back to the mother church and is now displayed in the Cenacle.

The Marian year of 1954 brought awakening of interest in Caversham's ancient shrine and the

then parish priest, Fr. William O'Malley, decided that a suitable shrine, reminiscent of the medieval chapel, should be built.

A magnificent statue of Mary, nursing the infant Christ, carved from a single block of oak and believed to be 500 years old, was purchased from an antique shop in London and blessed in December 1955. The foundation stone fashioned from stones of the original chapel is simply inscribed "Jesus-Maria" and a cavity contains coins of the realm and of the Vatican state, a portrait of the late Pope Pius XII, a newspaper of the day and a list of names of parishioners who helped to prepare the site where the shrine now stands. The west arch of the chapel features a screen of wrought iron, embellished with the arms of historic personages connected with the former history of the shrine. The renewed shrine was blessed and dedicated in 1959.

In 1996, the centenary of the first post-Reformation Mass in Caversham was celebrated with the crowning of the medieval statue. A crown of silver and gold was taken to Rome in May of that

year to be blessed by Pope John Paul II. On 20th July 1996 it was ceremoniously placed upon the head of the statue by the Papal Nuncio thus completing the link with the medieval shrine.

St. Anne's School and Convent

St. Anne's School, on the corner of Washington Road and Southview Avenue, was established in 1899 and was initially run by lay teachers. An inspection report dated March 1902 indicates that there was cause for concern and the parish priest, Fr. Wells, invited the Visitation Sisters from Belgium to come in order to bring *stability and organisation to the school.*

Under the leadership of Sr. Margaret Mary and the guidance of the Visitation Sisters, the school thrived and in 1909 inspectors wrote: *The influence of the Headteacher is excellent and the tone of the school is very pleasing. Good methods are followed and the level of intelligence and attainment is very satisfactory.* The good reputation of the school resulted in increased numbers and in the 1920s and 1930s the school was extended.

The Firs soon proved to be inadequate for the expanding community of nuns and so a new convent was built situated between the school and the church. This was extended in the 1930s when a chapel was built on the west side of the convent. The convent garden boasted an orchard, the fruits of which provided many a reward for *good work.*

The Sisters were also much involved in the pastoral life of the parish as well as providing the full complement of staff for the school. Their significant contribution to the life of the parish is much appreciated.

By 2005 the number of sisters had dwindled and the Sisters of the Visitation took the painful decision to close the convent. The building was bought by developers and has been converted into apartments.

Saint Anne's Well

Although the medieval shrine was destroyed in 1538, the well escaped. In 1906 some brickwork was discovered when workmen found a circular ancient well. Its depth had not been ascertained but there were signs that a heading had been driven to tap a spring, inferring that water was sufficiently near the surface for dipping. Historians inform us that there were a number of wells dedicated to St. Anne throughout the country.

Why so many? In pagan times people came to these wells and they had become surrounded by superstitious worship.

© John R Mullaney

Prayer to Our Lady of Caversham

All-holy Mother of God, who in the ages of Faith received in this place the veneration of our fathers, pray for us that we may grow in God's grace and be led to the knowledge and love of your Divine Son, who with the Father and the Holy Spirit lives and reigns world without end.

Amen.

Here were the gods, as it were, supplying them with fresh water from the bowels of the earth. When the country was converted, the church dedicated the wells to St. Anne as the English word Ann or Anna means brook or water. In 1378, Pope Urban authorised devotion to St.Anne and the well of St. Anne in Caversham became the scene of many pilgrimages with the waters reported to have effected many cures. The well is situated on Priest Hill, allegedly so called because of the number of religious making their way in procession at certain times to the well.

CHAPTER 6

A Visit to English Martyrs Parish

A New Parish

We must thank Father Kernan for his faith that the parish of St James was destined to grow, and specifically that its western area would grow significantly. From late 1921 there was a temporary church, an old army hut, to serve the worshipping community that already foresaw a church dedicated to the English Martyrs. It was a convert, Reginald Cecil Lybbe Powys-Lybbe, whose generous donation made the building of the church possible. This was opened on the 14th of September 1926, and in 1935 the parish formally separated from its mother church of St James.

Inside the Church

Once inside, notice the crucifix on the wall on the left-hand side of the altar. This came from the Carmelite Monastery which was located in Southcote Road. The Carmel was officially established on the 10th of June 1926, in a house bought for the purpose. At first the sisters earned their living by making vestments, but later they switched to providing altar breads. Although the sisters were totally enclosed the chapel was open to parishioners. Falling numbers caused the decision to close the monastery in 1998.

At the right-hand side of the church is a chapel, separated from the main church by heavy glass doors. The stained glass in the doors came from Presentation College which was situated on Bath Road. Between 1931 and 2004 the College provided a Catholic grammar school education for boys. Under the 11 plus, places at Presentation College were reserved for Catholic boys from Berkshire.

This continued from 1956 to 1980 when it became an independent school. The school is now closed.

The building of the chapel, originally intended as a baptistery, was not part of the original design of the church. It was part of the additional work carried out in 1970 which also provided the Community Centre, the presbytery and the linking colonnade. During the week the Community Centre is the home of *English Martyrs Pre-School*, set up by parishioners as *English Martyrs Playgroup* in 1972.

The Convent

With the building of the new presbytery, the former presbytery, number 62 Liebenrood Road, became the home of the Assumption Sisters, who had begun work in the parish in 1969. They visited the sick and housebound and instructed children not at Catholic schools.

They set up a group for teenagers, arranging talks, dramatic productions and retreats.

Some of the sisters were among the first Extraordinary Ministers of Holy Communion. They also worked in local schools and Battle Hospital.

In May 1984 the sisters moved to 70 Southcote Lane, a small House belonging to the Presentation Brothers. Here they continued their parish work.

Two years later, in 1986, they were asked to help a sister house in Lochyside. In order to do this it became necessary to close the Reading house, although a visiting sister continues to come to the parish to give retreats.

The Calvary in the grounds of the church.

In the background the house which over the years served as a presbytery and later became the Convent of the Sisters of the Assumption

A Meditation

When English Martyrs' Church was opened on the 14th of September 1926, the sermon was preached by Fr Edward Rockliffe SJ.
He reminded the congregation that the English Martyrs stood for principles they believed to be absolutely sacred, and that it was thanks to them that the Faith was never entirely torn out of this land.
Let us thank not only the saints whose names we know, but all those known only to God, who worked, suffered and even died to preserve the Faith for our generation.

The artwork over the main altar, which was specially commissioned for the church, depicts the Last Supper.

The shadow is intentional and represents the Barque of Peter.

Catholic Education

In the colonnade you will see the notice board showing the parish activities and you may also find colourful display material or brochures relating to the two schools in the parish area: English Martyrs' Primary School and Blessed Hugh Faringdon Catholic School.

The 1944 Education Act provided free schooling for all children, with separate provision for primary and secondary pupils.

Denominational religious education could only be provided in *Voluntary Aided* schools. To be classed as such the cost of building the school had to met by the church.

The English Martyrs School

This opened in 1957 in the newly built St Joseph's Centre in Tilehurst with Sister Anselm as its head. The school building on Dee Road, paid for by the efforts of parishioners, was completed at the end of 1961 and the school moved in on the 16th of January 1962.

The following April it became English Martyrs Voluntary Aided Primary School, with Sr. Anselm as head. She retired in 1982.

Over the years the original eight-classroom school has been extended, most recently in 2011 with two new classrooms.

The school continues to provide the Catholic education for which parishioners in the past worked so hard.

The Blessed Hugh Faringdon Catholic School and Sixth Form Centre

The school was built at a cost to the Catholic community of £200,000, while Reading Borough Council had to pay £16,000.

Even when the school opened, in April 1958, it was obvious that it was too small. Since then it has been extended, with English Martyrs, among other parishes, contributing to the cost. Blessed Hugh Faringdon Catholic School, as it is now known, continues to serve the Catholic community in the greater Reading area and provides education through to Sixth Form.

Hugh Faringdon Window in English Martyrs Church

CHAPTER 7

The Catholic Community of St Joseph's in Tilehurst

The story of the Catholic community of Tilehurst is that of the time, generosity and effort of ordinary people achieving extraordinary results, out of love for their neighbour and their Faith.

A WALK AROUND TILEHURST

Allow I hour walking time

1. Former home of Mr and Mrs Eppstein.
2. Village Hall.
3. St Joseph's Church.
4. First priest's house, 2, Firs Rd.
5. Fox and Hounds.

© John R Mullaney

The Eppstein House and Mass Centre

1. Former home of the Eppsteins.

Our walk begins at the large house on the corner in Kentwood Close, home in the 1930s of a Catholic couple called the Eppsteins. They offered their house as a Mass venue; a collapsible altar was made with the help of the local coffin-maker, and monthly Masses began. But by 1941 the Catholic population of Tilehurst had grown too big - 67 crammed into the house on one occasion - and it was time to find somewhere bigger.

Leave Kentwood Close and turn left into Kentwood Hill. At the traffic lights, turn right into Armour Road and first left into Victoria Road. A little way along, on the left, you come to Tilehurst Village Hall.

2. Village Hall

This was where local Catholics went to Mass for the next 15 years. There were only the floorboards to kneel on, and week by week the altar had to be put up and taken down again. Despite these discomforts, the Catholic population continued to grow, and by the early 1950s it was clear that Tilehurst would have to have a proper church of its own.

The parish priest of English Martyrs in the early 1950s, Father William Kirk, started a big fund-raising effort which included whist drives and a weekly football pool. The landlord of the Wheatsheaf Inn in Friar Street, Captain Capelli, donated the rough patch of land next to a pig farm on which the church now stands. The building, now the parish hall, was completed in under a year and cost less than £10,000. It was also used as a schoolroom – a curtain divided the main hall into two classes, with a third in the small hall downstairs, which was added for the purpose.

Tilehurst Village Hall

Continue down Victoria Road to the T-junction, turn left into Westwood Road, and right at the end into School Road. Continue past the shops for about half a mile (by which time School Road has become Park Lane) until you reach Berkshire Drive. Enter St Joseph's via the pedestrian gate on the opposite corner.

3. St Joseph's Church

4 First Priest's House

1n 1964, a curate from English Martyrs, Fr Scantlebury, was given responsibility for Tilehurst, and he moved into a bungalow further up Park Lane, 2 Firs Road, that had been left to the church by a Miss Kernan. Two years later Fr Scantlebury was replaced by Tilehurst's first parish priest, the redoubtable Colm Kelleher. He stayed for 33 years, nearly every week urging his congregations to put more in the collection plate. Within 5 years the parish was in a position to fund the building of a primary school, St Paul's in City Road.

After another seven years of scrimping and saving there was enough for the new church, down the slope from the first one, and a purpose-built presbytery.

St Joseph's is now amalgamated with English Martyrs and forms the new parish of English Martyrs and St Joseph.

The house is used every day by the many dedicated volunteers who – like their parish predecessors – give their love and time to make sure St Joseph's continues to thrive.

5. The Fox and Hounds

Father Colm Kelleher

Our walk ends here, but if you wish to extend it you can continue up Park Lane and turn right into City Road. You will pass St Paul's School on your left, and after the bend in the road, the Fox and Hounds pub which a wartime evacuee remembers being used for Mass in about 1940.

THE FONT — A MEDITATION

The font, installed in 2009, represents a trinity of trinities.

✝ The idea came from a group of parishioners; the base was carved by artist Richard Bray and the bowl by Reading stonemason AF Jones.

✝ It evokes the tree of life, the new life of Baptism and upheld muscled arms holding the world in its hands.

✝ The yew trunk divides into three: the Father, the Son and the Holy Spirit, by whom those being baptised are blessed.

Father, Son and Holy Spirit inspire us. Hold us in your hands. Give us your blessings. Amen.

CHAPTER 8

The Parish of Christ The King

Beginnings

Up until 1946 Whitley was part of St James' parish. As the Catholic population of Whitley grew, with the expansion of the area, it was recognised that there was a need for a local church. From 1928 Mass had been celebrated in an old army hut, by priests from St James'.

The Church of Christ the King

In 1946 Father Patrick Collins came to Whitley to be the first Parish Priest. There was no presbytery so he lodged with parishioners. By this time the old hut was too small for the growing congregation. An additional new Mass centre was opened in the scout hut in Callington Rd.

Before long the parish had outgrown that Mass centre. It was decided to use the large hall in the South Reading Community Centre. During this time Father Collins made contact with the prisoner of war camp in Whitley Wood Road.

Each Sunday Catholic POWs were allowed to attend Mass at which they led the singing. Father Collins also encouraged parishioners to invite the POWs into their homes for lunch.

Cressingham Road

The population of Whitley continued to increase so eventually a temporary church-cum-hall, with an attached flat for the priest, was built in Cressingham Road by the people of the area, Catholic and otherwise. This building was to serve the parish for many years. In 1954 it became an annexe to St James' School, with two classrooms.

The Opening of the New Church

Father Collins 'had a dream' to purchase land to build a permanent church. The parishioners were not well off but they generously gave what they could. The foundation stone was laid by Archbishop John Henry King in 1958. The following year the church of Christ the King was consecrated by the Abbot of Douai and the first Mass was celebrated on the 6th of December, 1959.

The Sanctuary of Christ the King Church

Inside the Church

The church has a simple and dignified layout. The organ is particularly fine.

Father Patrick Collins was truly a man of the people, who touched many lives. He was much missed when he died in 1970. He was a generous man who lived frugally and gave what he had to those in most need.

Christ the King School

In 1967 the primary school of Christ the King was opened and the children of Whitley had their own school.

When St James' School closed down on the 28th June 1968 the pupils transferred to Christ the King. Today Christ the King school is very much at the heart of the life of the parish.

Today the parish of Christ the King, built on the prayers and efforts of the past, is a vibrant, multicultural community. There are parishioners from many countries including Goa, the Philippines, Poland, many countries of Africa and South America as well as Ireland and the British Isles.

It has an excellent choir which sings at the Sunday morning Mass and dedicated catechists who lead the children's Sunday liturgy as well as prepare children for the Sacraments.

There is a club for the over 60s. Parishioners are actively involved in the many ministries of the church and its outreach in the local community.

CHAPTER 9

St John Bosco. Our Lady of Peace and Blessed Dominic Barberi.

Beginnings

Although today these are two separate parishes, the story of Catholicism in Woodley and Earley is complex and interwoven.

In the early 19th century Woodley Lodge, the home of James Wheble, was an important Mass centre for local Catholics before the building of St James' church. This latter then became the parish church for the whole of Reading until the building of St William of York in 1906 to serve the eastern parts of the town.

Mass was also celebrated, among other places, in Earley St Peter's church hall, at Reading Cricket Club, and in the East Lodge of the Bulmershe estate.

The old East Lodge of Bulmershe Court

said in a hall, belonging to a printer, in Crockhamwell Road, and this was later used as a church hall and a presbytery. For a time there was a private convent school, also dedicated to St John Bosco, and run by the Sisters of Mercy, on the same site but this moved to Farrier's Close and eventually closed in 1981. A parish primary school, Saint Dominic Savio's, opened in Western Avenue in 1966 and continues to flourish.

St John Bosco Parish

In 1946 a new parish, dedicated to St John Bosco, was set up to serve Woodley, Sonning and Earley. The East Lodge was extended to provide a church, using voluntary labour and the services of some Polish builders who had been living in a camp in Nettlebed. It was opened on the 3rd of October 1948. During the building work Mass was

The interior of the first St John Bosco Church

The New Parish Church

In 1966 developers bought the site of the first parish church, the parish hall and the original convent in order to build Crockhamwell Road shopping precinct. For a time Mass was celebrated in the hall of St Dominic Savio Primary School until the present church of St John Bosco was completed. It opened in the summer of 1970.

St John Bosco Parish Church

Shortly after his arrival at St John Bosco's in 2005, Fr Chris Whelan noticed that there were no consecration crosses in the church.

Further enquiries at the diocesan office confirmed that there was no record of the church ever having been consecrated. The parish took steps to put matters right, and finally, 37 years after it opened its doors, the church was consecrated by Bishop Crispian Hollis on Sunday, the 4th of March, 2007.

Our Lady of Peace and Blessed Dominic Barberi

Mass at Our Lady of Peace

In 1972 the area south of the Reading to Waterloo railway line ceased to be part of Woodley parish.

A possible site for a new church had been purchased at Earley crossroads in 1950, when there was talk of merging St John Bosco and St William of York parishes. When this plan was shelved the site was used to erect a hall and eventually, in 1972, to build the new church of Our Lady of Peace Blessed Dominic Barberi, which opened in June 1976.

Earley's first parish priest was Father Vincent Flanagan, who extended the original hall into a community centre and social club, opened in 1980 by Bishop Emery.

Father Flanagan's successor, Father Peter Codd, hoped to found a new parish, dedicated to Blessed Dominic Barberi, in the massive new housing estate of Lower Earley. Father Codd, who lived in Sawtry Close, celebrated Sunday Mass, for a time, in Loddon Valley Primary School.

However the church of Blessed Dominic Barberi was never built as it was decided to amalgamate the Lower Earley parish with Our Lady of Peace.

This explains why the church at Earley Crossroads is called *Our Lady of Peace and Blessed Dominic Barberi*. The amalgamated parish of Our Lady of Peace and Blessed Dominic Barberi came into being in 1990.

The Church of Our Lady of Peace and Blessed Dominic Barberi

Fr Eamon Walsh, who was the parish priest from 1993 to 2004, was a pivotal influence in building a new extension which was added onto the front of the church.

This has given more space at busy times and more flexibility for courses and meetings. The new room was opened in 2003 and was officially named *The Advent Room*. The parish continues to have strong ties with the neighbouring churches of St. John Bosco and Christ the King. It describes itself as *indeed a place enriched by people from near and far,* with between thirty and forty different nationalities regularly attending Mass.

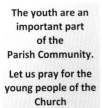

The youth are an important part of the Parish Community.

Let us pray for the young people of the Church

CHAPTER 10

The Polish Community in Reading

Reading's large Polish community now worships at Sacred Heart Church in Watlington Street. However, its origins lie to the north of Reading, at Checkendon, where, from 1948 until the early 1960s there was a large Polish Hostel, or Camp, created to house displaced Polish families who had, in some cases, spent up to eight years in exile in Russia, Iran, Lebanon, India and Africa before being allowed to settle in England.

Corpus Christi procession at Checkendon Camp

Accommodation was in very basic Nissen huts, without water, sanitation or proper heating. Two families shared each hut. Despite the deprivations of life in the camp many former residents look back at their time there with nostalgia.

Central to the life of the camp was the Chapel, also in a Nissen hut, where the priest, Father Botor, and later Father Nowak, celebrated Mass.

One former resident says that the Church helped Polish people survive the horrors of the war years and gave colour to the

somewhat bleak conditions in the camp and was in so many ways the focal point of life for the community.

The year was punctuated by festivals such as Corpus Christi, when a procession wound its way around the camp, whatever the weather, First Holy Communions and visits from Polish prelates and dignitaries such as General Anders, commander of the 2nd Polish Corps and a prominent member of the Polish Government in Exile. Adults from the camp would travel by bus to work at factories in Oxford or Reading, including Huntley and Palmers.

Children were educated at

local primary schools or at a Polish school set up in Checkendon.

As they grew older the young people went to local secondary schools or were sent away to Polish boarding schools, both grammars and secondary moderns. Many became teachers or entered other professions. Gradually the camp emptied as families moved into their own houses and in the early 1960s the camp was closed.

For many years the Reading Polish community attended Mass at St James' church. Then in 1981 came the chance to buy St John's, a former

Anglican church. The church was consecrated by Cardinal Rubin on 5th December 1981 and dedicated to the Sacred Heart of Jesus as an expression of gratitude for the preservation of the Polish community. The stained glass windows from the Nissen hut chapel were installed in the church next to the altar as a permanent memorial of the early years in Britain.

The Corpus Christi procession sets off from Sacred Heart Church

Many Polish traditions are still observed at the Sacred Heart Church. On Holy Saturday beautifully decorated baskets are brought into church to be blessed by the priest.

They always include coloured hard boiled eggs, bread, salt, often grated horseradish, and small samples of the food to be served the following day for Easter lunch. The centrepiece is a figure of the Easter lamb, sometimes made of marzipan or painted plaster, carrying the banner of triumph over death

and standing in a 'field' of fresh greenery. The basket is lined with a white lace-edged napkin and decorated with sprigs of box, signifying new life. The decorative 'palm' from Palm Sunday may also be included.

The baskets are arranged around the altar steps and sprinkled with Holy Water, after prayers referring to the Gospel significance of all the items and stressing the concept of rebirth. Naturally there is great competition as to who can produce the most artistic basket.

At Corpus Christi there is a colourful procession through the streets of Reading. Banners are carried by young people in national costume or Polish scout and guide uniform and children scatter rose petals before

the Blessed Sacrament.

Until recently, Benediction was held in the Abbey Ruins but now St James' church again welcomes the community for Benediction at the end of the procession.

The Sacred Heart church has recently completed extensive renovation and its white spire is a striking landmark on the Reading horizon.

Many of today's Polish community in Reading came here as economic migrants in the years following the end of Communist rule, and are firmly embedded in local society.

However the Sacred Heart church continues to provide a vibrant link to their mother country and a reminder of the crucial role played by the Catholic Church in the birth of modern Poland.

CHAPTER 11

Catholic Country Estates Around Reading

Throughout the years after the Reformation in the 16th century to be a Catholic risked imprisonment and even death. However, many of the country estates around Reading stayed in Catholic hands. Reading was a very Protestant town yet it was surrounded by these Catholic family houses which gave shelter to the few Catholics in the area and to the priests, mainly Franciscans, who served them.

Woodley Lodge

To the east of Reading, Woodley Lodge was the home of James Wheble, the founder of St James' Church in Reading. The Lodge no longer exists. It was demolished to make way for Bulmershe Teacher Training College.

James Wheble bought the estate in 1801. He became a leading figure in the history of Catholicism in Reading. His last chaplain, Father Ringrose, was the first priest in charge of St James'. It is also thanks to Wheble that A.W.N. Pugin was engaged as the architect of St James' Church.

Today the estate lies within the boundaries of the Parish of St John Bosco.

James Wheble 1779 –1840

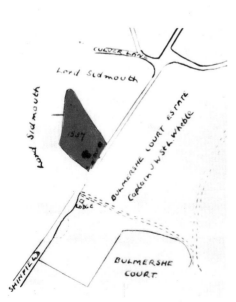

The red shaded area is the likely position of the house provided for Wheble's first chaplain, the Reverend Blardière, mentioned in the Cowslade Manuscript. He bequeathed his chalice to St James' as a token of gratitude to the Wheble family and to the Catholic community of Reading. The chalice is still kept in the church and it is a tangible reminder of the close connection between those who, like Blardière, struggled to keep the Faith alive during difficult times, and the Catholic community of today.

44

The Whiteknights Estate

This estate had been owned by the Englefield family since 1606. Sir Francis Englefield sold it to George Spencer, Marquis of Blandford, later Duke of Marlborough, in 1798.

According to the Cowslade Manuscript, an account of the history of Catholicism in Reading written in the 1840s, Sir Francis moved from his main family home *in disgust at the offensive prejudices of the neighbouring Gentry,* taking with him the chapel furnishings and vestments.

Whiteknights c 1800   Courtesy of Reading Library

These were passed on to the new chapel in Finch's Buildings where Fr. Longuet and the French priests were ministering to the growing Catholic population. Many of these items were then transferred to the Chapel of the Resurrection in 1812.

The site is now the University of Reading and is freely accessible. Nothing remains of the house, though the lake shown in the picture is still there.

Ufton Court

In one way or another Ufton Court had been in the Perkins family from before the Reformation and throughout the penal times. During the reign of Elizabeth I the family risked martyrdom by hiding priests in the house. As late as the mid 1700s it is said that Charles Stuart visited the house after the failure of the '45 Jacobite rebellion.

After Francis Englefield sold Whiteknights the Franciscan priest, Father Baynham, came to Ufton Court. He was one of the few English priests who served the people of Reading before the arrival of the French clergy. He occasionally said Mass in the Minster Street room rented by Mrs Smart.

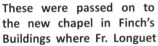

Ufton Court c. 1820

Courtesy of Reading Library

Today Ufton court is used as an educational centre.

Mapledurham House and the Blount Family

The Two Chapels

The Catholic chapel in Mapledurham House dates from the 1790s, following the 1791 Catholic Relief Act which permitted such places of worship once again, provided there was no steeple or bell.

This chapel, dedicated to St. Michael, marks a climax in achievement since the days when the house was first built in 1588. It is possibly the only recusant house built with its own chapel and hiding places for priests as these were usually achieved by alterations.

The Secret Chapel with its cluster of oyster shells

Secret Signs and Priest Holes

When built, its purpose is thought to have been to provide a safe house for priests after Stonor Park had been raided and lost its security. The secret chapel at Mapledurham was hidden away at the top of the house, with hiding holes close by. Priests would probably come and go by river and there is a cluster of oyster shells over a window facing the river to assist in guiding the stranger.

This carried on for two hundred years, with the family being fined and suffering many restrictions such as being excluded from public life, the army and professions and also from voting. Catholics were only allowed to keep one horse.

Despite all these restrictions, life seems to have carried on quite peacefully and generally harmoniously with neighbours. Mapledurham does not seem to have been raided as other recusant houses were, although there is a report of an escape from a house beside the Thames.

The Civil War and the Siege of Reading

During the Civil War most recusant Catholics were Royalists. Michael Blount helped to defend Reading during the siege. Indeed he raised the siege by sending barges down river to Reading with provisions. During another siege, Mapledurham was attacked and damaged, although it was not taken. Later the estate was sequestrated for a few years.

Tolerance and Growth

Mapledurham was able to give succour to other Catholics and gradually the small congregation outgrew the secret chapel. Then a larger chapel was made and in 1743 Catholics felt secure enough to keep a chapel register. Around this time Alexander Pope is known to have frequented Mapledurham and Reading Catholics, such as the Smart family, attended Mass here.

Revolution

But the great change seems to have been at the time of the French Revolution, when Reading gave hospitality to many priests and others fleeing the continent. With the relaxing of the anti-Catholic laws, in 1791, the present chapel could be built, giving much more room and access from outside, beside Saint Margaret's Parish Church.

By this time the family was much impoverished but it was important to furnish the chapel suitably in the new Strawberry Hill Gothick style which it retains today. Copies of well known religious pictures were hung on the walls, although there were no foundations and the exterior appeared as domestic offices.

Catholic Emancipation

In 1829 the Catholic Emancipation Act was passed. It is interesting that Michael Blount was then nominated to be High Sheriff. However the priests who lived at Mapledurham had a very hard life as is illustrated by their letters of complaint.

In 1830 there were three schools in tiny Mapledurham, with Mrs. Blount running one of them.

The Churches of St James and St Anne

In 1840 St. James' was built and took over the supporting role that Mapledurham had provided. Our Lady and St. Anne's church, in Caversham, would follow.

After Michael Blount died in 1874, the house was let, but the chapel was lovingly cared for by two Miss Blounts who lived at Rose Farm and every day they tended the chapel.

The 18th Century Chapel

The Twentieth Century

During the 1st World War a community of nuns were evacuated to Mapledurham. After the war, Edward Riddell-Blount lived there and maintained the chapel.

There were annual Corpus Christi processions from Our Lady and St. Anne's. Parishioners walked out from Caversham, while a Salters steamer brought those who could not walk.

The chapel gradually fell into abeyance during and after the 2nd World War but had a brief resurgence when Lord and Lady Rankeillou re-established Mass for a few years.

When the house was restored, in the 1960s, the chapel was also completely renovated with a most substantial grant from the Historic Building Council without which it could not have been saved.

Since its rededication by Archbishop Dwyer Mass has been celebrated in the chapel on a regular basis.

Exterior of the 18th century chapel

CHAPTER 12

The Martyrdom of Hugh Cook of Faringdon, 14th November 1539

Trial and Execution

Abbot Hugh was the 31st Abbot of Reading. He shared his name with the first abbot who had been appointed 400 years earlier. In 1539 Abbot Hugh was accused of treason for refusing to surrender the Abbey to the Crown.

Thomas Cromwell wrote that the order was issued that Abbot Hugh was to be *tried and executed for* treason.

Along with John Eynon and John Rugge, two of his fellow monks, he was imprisoned in the Tower and finally brought to Reading to be tried.

Hugh denied his guilt to the last. No evidence of malpractice was ever brought against Reading Abbey.

At the trial, where he was allowed no defence, he was accused of denying the supremacy of Henry as Head of the Church in England.

The trial was held in the manorial court over the Inner Gateway to the Abbey, next to his own Abbot's House, on the 14th or 15th of November.

Abbot Hugh Cook of Faringdon

The jury consisted of local gentry whom he must have known well, many of them being long-standing tenants of the Abbey.

Having been sentenced, Abbot Hugh was stretched out and tied to a hurdle, then dragged through the streets of Reading. It was reported that crowds gathered all along the way. Many spat at him and threw excrement.

He was sentenced to be put to death by hanging, drawing and quartering.

In this form of punishment the prisoner was hanged, but in such a way as to leave him conscious. The spinal cord was not broken, so allowing the disembowelling and cutting up of the body to be done whilst the prisoner was still alive.

However, either because the executioner was incompetent, or because he took pity on the Abbot, Hugh died when he was hanged.

John Rugge and John Eynon were subsequently also executed.

THE ROUTE OF ABBOT HUGH'S MARTYRDOM

1. The Abbey Gateway. 2. New Strete (Friar St). 3. Gutter Lane (Cross St).
4. Broad St. 5. Chayne Lane (Chain St). 6. Old Strete (The Butts).
7. Seaven Bridges (Bridge St). 8. St Giles Strete (Southampton St).
9. Siever Strete (Silver St). 10. London St. 11. Shomakers Row (Market Place).
12. The Forbury. 13. The Gibbet (most probably in front of the Abbey Gateway).

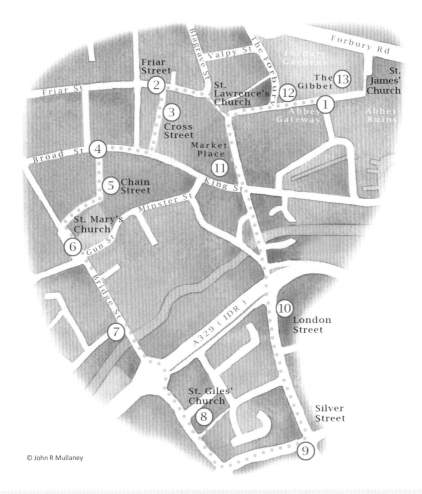

© John R Mullaney

If you choose to follow this trail, and as you pass through the bustling streets of modern Reading, consider how this monk, about 475 years ago, was mocked by the crowd and murdered for his Faith.

Today the town's Catholic Secondary school is named after him and we honour him as a martyr of the Church.

CONTACTS

If you intend visiting any of the parishes mentioned and would like to check times when the churches are open we suggest you phone in advance. We are giving a selection of the phone numbers of the main places mentioned in the booklet. You can of course find out more by visiting their respective websites.

ST JAMES AND ST WILLIAM OF YORK	0118 957 4171
OUR LADY AND ST ANNE'S CAVERSHAM	0118 947 1787
ENGLISH MARTYRS AND ST JOSEPH'S	0118 957 2149
CHRIST THE KING	0118 931 4469
OUR LADY OF PEACE AND BLESSED DOMINIC BARBERI	0118 966 3711
ST JOHN BOSCO	0118 969 3423
THE SACRED HEART CHURCH	0118 957 3647
MAPLEDURHAM HOUSE	0118 972 3350

We should like to remind those going on the walks that some of the places mentioned in the book are private properties and we ask that you should respect the privacy of their owners.

ACKNOWLEDGEMENTS

In addition to the contributors mentioned in the *Contents* we are most grateful to Ann Davis and Simon Harrington for their thorough and invaluable proof reading.

We wish to thank Mrs Patricia Rolt for her memories of the history of Christ the King and Chris Kent for the information about Bulmershe Court.

This information about English Martyrs is from the *Red Brick Church* series of four books produced to celebrate the 75th anniversary of the opening of English Martyrs' church, in particular from articles contributed by Catherine Harrington and John Whitehead. Material on the different religious communities was drawn from articles contributed anonymously and published in the books under the title "In their own words". All photographs were taken by Pat Walsh who maintains a photo archive of English Martyrs parish.

Linda Heneghan contributed information about the Irish community and the Irish Centre.

John R Mullaney gave advice on design and layout throughout the book.

Anna Zygalska-Cannon contributed a photograph and information about Polish Easter customs.

Further information about the history of Catholicism in Reading may be found in the book *Reformation, Revolution and Rebirth* by John Mullaney and Lindsay Mullaney.

Finally special thanks to Canon John O'Shea, whose idea it was to promote the publication of this pilgrimage book to mark the Year of Faith, and to the priests of Reading who supported him in this unique venture.

YEAR OF FAITH 2012 2013

The Confraternity of Saint James

The Confraternity of Saint James was established as a non-denominational association in 1983 by a group of six people who had made the pilgrimage, and wanted "to give something back", by giving help and advice to new generations of pilgrims: this remains their main purpose. More than thirty years down the line, they have some 2000 members. They publish a quarterly Bulletin for members and a series of guides to the pilgrim routes, available from the online bookshop. Their website also offers a library with an on-line catalogue, and a digital image collection. In partnership with Spanish Associations the Confraternity runs two pilgrim hostels in northwest Spain, at Rabanal del Camino and Miraz in Galicia. In the UK they organise a full programme of events.

In 2011 the Confraternity visited St James' in the Forbury and the CSJ Choir and others performed a *Pilgrimage Cantata* composed by John Read, illustrated with pictures of the Camino.

Several members of the Confraternity live around Reading. St James' Parish and the Confraternity are forging ever closer links and are working together to promote the various Caminos and to support those who wish to discover
what it means to be a pilgrim.

Icon in the library of the Refugio Gaucelmo, Rabanal.

Courtesy of the
Confraternity of Saint James.

Memorial icon made by Sister Petra Clare, for Stephen Badger, showing scenes from the life of St James and other events associated with the pilgrimage to Santiago, including Stephen and his family as pilgrims, with the Portico de la Gloria at the top of the picture.

For more information about the Confraternity, including the St James' Way Walk
visit their website www.csj.org.uk or phone 020 7928 9988

Scallop Shell Press

Ever since the Middle Ages the scallop shell has been the symbol of those going on pilgrimage to the shrine of Saint James in Compostela, Spain.

Today the pilgrimage is even more popular than ever as people of all faiths, and none, seek a meaning for their journey through life.

The shell became a metaphor for this journey, the grooves representing the many ways of arriving at one's destination. At a practical level the shell was also useful for scooping up water or food.

Scallop Shell Press aims to publish works which will offer the modern pilgrim stories of our shared humanity and help readers arrive at their own meaningful interpretations of life.

We hope that our books will be shells within whose covers readers will find an intellectual and spiritual source of sustenance for their own personal pilgrimage

If you would like to find out more about Scallop Shell Press then please visit our website
www.Scallopshellpress.co.uk   *or use our QR code*

Email: Scallopshellpress@yahoo.co.uk